The Family

God's

Masterpiece

HELEN D. BAUGH

Stonecroft, Inc.
10121 Grandview Road
Kansas City, Missouri 64137

*To my
son and daughter
and
their families
who are a joy to me.*

PREFACE

In a time when society is approving the philosophy of every man doing that which is right in his own eyes, it is important that we discover again God's plan for man through the family.

On the following pages the reader will learn what God's Word says about the family and its members. Here, too, are practical examples of how God's principles really work when applied to our every day lives.

It is our prayer that this book will help many to get their perspective "in focus" as Jesus Christ becomes the "Center" of their lives.

Mary E. Clark

Stonecroft 1975

Marriage Service

We are assembled here in the presence of God to join this man and this woman in holy marriage; which is instituted of God, regulated by His commandments, blessed by our Lord Jesus Christ, and to be held in honor among all men.

William, wilt thou have this woman to be thy wife, and wilt thou pledge thy troth to her, in all love and honor, in all duty and service, in all faith and tenderness, to live with her, and cherish her, according to the ordinance of God, in the holy bond of marriage?

Nancy, wilt thou have this man to be thy husband, and wilt thou pledge thy troth to him, in all love and honor, in all duty and service, in all faith and tenderness, to live with him, and cherish him, according to the ordinance of God, in the holy bond of marriage?

I, William, take thee, Nancy, to be my wedded wife; and I do promise and covenant, before God and these witnesses, to be thy loving and faithful husband, in plenty and in want, in joy and in sorrow, in sickness and in health, as long as we both shall live.

I, Nancy, take thee, William, to be my wedded husband; and I do promise and covenant, before God and these witnesses, to be thy loving and faithful wife, in plenty and in want, in joy and in sorrow, in sickness and in health, as long as we both shall live.

This ring I give thee, in token and pledge of our constant faith and abiding love.

By the authority committed unto me as a minister of Christ, I declare William and Nancy are now husband and wife, according to the ordinance of God and the law of the State, in the name of the Father, and of the Son, and of the Holy Spirit. Amen.

Whom, therefore, God hath joined together, let no man put asunder.

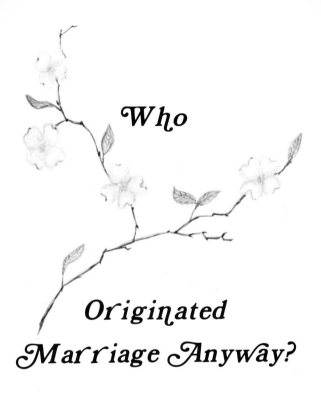

Who

Originated
Marriage Anyway?

Almost every little girl in America dreams of the day her "Prince Charming" will appear. There will be that beautiful day when she will float down the aisle in a "dream" of a dress - and they will live happily ever after.

Yet today almost 50% of the marriages in America end in divorce. As one young woman exclaimed, "Who would have thought that I'd ever be the third wife of my second husband!"

In one of our mid-west cities a young couple had just returned from their honeymoon. Seated at the breakfast table, the starry-eyed bride announced, "Today I'm going out and squander $5.00!"

But there was a rude awakening when her handsome bridegroom said rather sternly, "Let's get this straight once and for all. There will be *no* squandering of *any* amount of money in this family."

Was this the man she had dated?

A young business man arrived home one evening to announce, "Well, we're taking our vacation the first two weeks of July this year."

"Oh, but Honey, the last time I talked with my parents I told them we'd meet them at the shore in August."

"But the company said we have to take our vacation in July."

"But I just can't miss being at the shore with my family! I'm so lonesome for them!"

"Ann, you and I are your family now, and we have to take our vacation when it is assigned. After all, I am one of the newest ones in the office, you know."

"Oh, so the company's going to run our life, is it?"

Was this marriage? Was this the man she had dated?

Who originated marriage, anyway? Would you be surprised to learn that it was God who originated it?

In the Book of Beginnings (known to most of us as the book of Genesis in the Bible) God began the human race through a marriage! First, He created the man, Adam. Then, the Bible says, God saw that it was not good for man to be alone, so He created a helper for him - Eve.[1] Made from the rib which God took from Adam's side, Eve was to be his true assistant.

Then God said to them, *"Be fruitful and multiply."*[2]

As you watch a lovely bride walk demurely down the aisle, then follow the beautiful and meaningful wedding ceremony, do you ever notice the words that the clergyman speaks? Did you realize that part of that wording comes directly from the Bible and that very first wedding! We read in the book of Genesis when God gave Eve to Adam, *"Therefore, shall a man leave his father and mother, and shall cleave unto his wife: and they shall be one flesh."* [3]

With that statement the pattern for marriage was set.

From then until today, God has continued to carry out His plan through the family. First, it was the family of Adam through which the human race was begun. Then through Noah's family the earth was replenished after the flood. Through Abraham's family the Jewish nation came into existence, and through the family of David, the great King of Israel, God gave to the world the Lord Jesus Christ.

Let us see how we can have a home and a family which God can bless.

Who Controls Your Marriage?

Marriage was the first human relationship God gave to man and it is a sacred trust. A successful marriage is built on the love, respect and commitment of a man and a woman to each other.

A wedding is a very special and sacred occasion, whether it is a simple ceremony or an elaborate affair. It is a time that both the bride and groom will look back to as a milestone in their lives. The bride may wear a plain cotton dress or the traditional satin and lace, but usually she is in white to declare to her groom and the world her purity. The groom looks his best, for he wants to let her know that he is capable of being her provider for the rest of her life.

Marriage means that a man and a woman pledge themselves to live together in love and unity "until death us do part" or for the rest of their lives. They build a happy and successful life together as they . . .

. . .believe in each other

. . .encourage each other

. . .support each other in
their convictions and standards

. . .face life together, with its joys
and sorrows, for better or for
worse.

When asked for a definition of love, a little child said, "Love is something that makes two people think they are pretty when no one else thinks so."

Marriage is a partnership in which both partners need to have the same goals and be under the direction of the same Controller.

Marriage is ordained of God. When both partners are in right relationship with Him, and under His direction, they have marriage at its best.

In His life on earth, Jesus Christ put His "stamp of approval" on marriage by attending the wedding in Cana and there performing His first recorded miracle. [4]

There are three types of marriage partnerships:

1. A marriage of a man and a woman who do not know God.
2. A marriage of a man and a woman where one knows God and one is not related to Him.
3. A marriage of a man and a woman who are both believers in the Lord Jesus Christ.

When the marriage partnership consists of two partners who do not know God, they may have a measure of happiness. However, they miss the third dimension of life which is the spiritual dimension.

In such a marriage, as time goes on, both are aware of a gnawing void in their lives which nothing seems to fill, not even their love for one another.

There is a remedy for such a situation. (See page 97.)

Then there is the marriage in which one partner is a Christian - a true believer in Jesus Christ - while the other partner has not yet made any commitment to Him. Immediately we can see that there is a problem! Here are two people trying to "pull together" when they are headed for two different destinations. The Bible says, *"Can two walk together, except they be agreed?"*[5] This is a very important consideration when two people are contemplating marriage.

Such a marriage can be transformed when the non-Christian partner comes to the place of trusting Christ. [6]

In the marriage between two partners who both love the Lord, there can be unity of purpose as each partner seeks to do the will of God. They look to Him for their directions and solutions, allowing Him to be in control of their lives and their marriage. This makes for "smooth sailing."

If you find yourself in classification one or two, there is a remedy. You can both be rightly related to God. That makes the difference!

A TRIBUTE TO MY WIFE
ON OUR WEDDING ANNIVERSARY
(by a minister)

Thank you, Dear,
for golden memories today. Memories
of those exciting months when our love
deepened and we waited with joy for the
holy encounter called marriage. Those
were fun days. Days when we laughed
and dreamed as only lovers can. And
they were days of uncertainty, when we
wondered about the future and were a
little fearful. But they were days, also,
when we began to learn that our times
are in His hand and that He orders and
directs our paths. It was then we began
to pray together and plan together and
think together of two lives together in
His will doing His work.

And I remember the wedding day.
What delightful confusion! It didn't
seem to matter to us that it rained all
day, that our plans went awry and that
the entire wedding party was late for the
ceremony. It didn't matter that your lit-
tle brother refused at the last minute to
"bear the rings" and that the musicians
had to cancel. What did matter was that

the Lord joined two people together with vows so strong and sacred that only death can bring release. We were there, you and I, in His presence - that's what mattered.

And I cannot forget your unselfishness - when you asked that I not give you a diamond so the money could go for school expense - when you shopped the bargain basements and stretched dollars and passed by pretty clothes and lived in cramped quarters and learned how to fix hamburger 100 exciting ways! I remember, too, the countless times you shared me with our people by canceling personal plans, waiting meals and urging me to pass you by for some other life in need.

Yes, I do remember and my heart is filled with gratitude.

Happy anniversary, Dear.

. .Excerpt from SOME FOLKS I KNOW by Wendell Grout

Who is Chairman of the Board?

God has ordained that the man is to be the head of the family under God. [7]   What a responsibility!

As the head of the family, the man is the PROVIDER.   All through the Bible, which, by the way, is the original "marriage manual," we see how the man has provided the shelter or home for his bride.   The bride leaves her family circle to be with her husband in the home he provides for her. That home spells security for her and the family which God gives to them.

As head of the family, the husband arranges for the financial security of his family. It takes money to provide food and clothing for those he loves. But father must never become just "the one who shells out the money." He is a loving provider who is concerned for all the needs of his family.

The husband also provides the emotional security needed by both his wife and children. They need to feel his love, expressed in many different ways. It is expressed through the provision of a good home, adequate food and clothing, an education. It is expressed by the time spent with the family - not always the quantity of time, but the quality of his interest in their activities. It might be expressed even in the fact that he cannot spend as much time with them as he would like. Perhaps he is using his time for further training or in additional work in order to provide their needs.

PROTECTOR. As head of the family, the father is the protector. The Bible tells us that husbands are to love their wives as Christ loves us. [8] Christ gave His life for us. So when a man loves his wife as much as Christ loves us, to the point of being willing even to give his life for her safety, there will be no thought in that man's mind of "cracking the whip" or "lording it over her."

The role of the male as protector is beautifully illustrated in the animal kingdom for God has placed this same instinct in them. Bird watchers tell of the male bird who "stakes out" an area as his own property and will fight any other male who dares to try to invade it. Then, when the female has been courted and won, the nest built and the eggs laid in it, the father bird again takes up his role as protector.

While mother bird sits patiently hour after hour warming the eggs, father flies out to bring back food for her. Darting here and there, he keeps a constant watch for enemies. A snake crawls along the limb of the tree and instantly father bird swoops down to take its attention away from the nest. A little boy, climbing the tree, gets too close for comfort to that little home. Father bird flies very close to little Sonny to startle him and take his attention in another direction.

Human fathers have the responsibility of protecting the family not only physically but mentally and spiritually, also. Dad will want to know what kinds of books the children are reading; what activities they participate in; who their friends are; what TV programs they are watching. Children accept what they hear as truth. Often these programs are presenting ideas and thoughts not in accord with your beliefs.

And, yes, father's protection will include loving discipline as he protects his children from themselves! In the Bible we read, *"For whom the Lord loves He corrects, even as a father corrects the son in whom he delights."*[9] And, *"Fathers, don't over-correct your children or make it difficult for them to obey the commandment. Bring them up with Christian teaching in Christian discipline."* [10]

The husband's protective instinct toward his wife means he will never speak discourteously of her before others nor embarrass her by his actions. He wants her to be his alone, that they might have the holy, righteous relationship which God ordained for one man and one woman.

All too often today, God's plan for marriage and the family is being broken down. Books and articles are being published encouraging women to have illicit relationships outside the home. Women are allowing other women to come between them and their husbands. Or the man thinks he can "have his cake and eat it too" through extra-marital affairs.

This is not NEW MORALITY; just the same OLD SIN. . .and it is NEVER sanctioned by God.

SPIRITUAL LEADER. As the head, the man is to be the spiritual leader of the family.

When God selected one family - the family of Abraham - through which to bless the entire race, He set the father as the priest of the family. It was the father who spoke to God for his family and to his family for God.

Today each person has the privilege of speaking to God directly, but the father still has the responsibility for the spiritual training of his children. God's instruction given in the Bible to fathers so long ago is still meant for fathers today:

> *"And you shall love the Lord your God with all your mind and heart, and with your entire being, and with all your might. And these words, which I am commanding you today, shall be [first] in your own mind and heart; [then] you shall whet and sharpen them, so as to make them penetrate, and teach and impress them diligently upon the minds and hearts of your children, and shall talk of them when you sit in your house, and when you walk by the way, and when you lie down and when you rise up."*[11]

All too often in our busy lives today, father has abdicated this place of responsibility. True, today's family schedules are "something else!"

Each member seems to have a schedule which conflicts with each of the others. Father goes to work at 8:00 in the morning, but some of the children have to catch the bus at 7:00. To get everyone up and ready for a time of family devotions in the morning seems next to impossible!

The evening meal time seems almost as hopeless. Dad has to work late - or go out of town - or have dinner with a customer. Son has football practice; daughter has piano lessons. . .and mother has to act as chauffeur! All too often our modern home is like a motel with a coffee shop - we just eat and sleep there!

But God still holds Dad responsible.

It is most important to establish a time when most, if not all, of the family are together to read God's Word and to pray. Perhaps this will be only a few minutes each day, but it will have a profound effect not only on your family relationships, but on the future life of your children. Then, at least once during the week, a time should be planned when all the family can be together to discuss the activities of each member and to relate this to God's plan for each life.

The Bible says: *"For now that you have faith in Christ Jesus you are all sons of God. Gone is the distinction between. . .male and female - you are all one in Christ Jesus."*[12]

Dad is the God-ordained head of the home and should be the spiritual leader, However, this phase of his responsibility may be difficult to carry out if he does not know the Lord in a personal way.

In such a case, the wife cannot expect her husband to give the family leadership in an area about which he has no knowledge. Should he make a decision that would be contrary to the Word of God, the wife would need to recognize that her first responsibility is to God.[13] She should follow the Lord's leading. She should remember, however, that there is a *gracious* way to do this without causing antagonism. It may not be easy, but through love and prayer and with an understanding heart, God will see her through these difficult years. In time, the Bible promises, her husband will come to know the Lord as he observes her life.[14]

RESULTS. As I finished speaking one day, a lovely woman stopped to talk with me before she left the room. There was a look of sadness about her eyes as she commented:

"Twenty years ago, when my husband insisted that he did not want me to go to church on Sundays, I decided to comply with his wishes. Perhaps, I thought, if I am gracious in this, he will soon change his mind.

"Time went on, however, and he didn't change.

"For the past 20 years, I have not attended church, although I longed to do so. Not only has my husband not come to Christ, but not

25

one of my children is a Christian. How I wish I had followed the Bible admonition, *'Not forsaking the assembling of yourselves together, as the manner of some is...'"* (Hebrews 10:25)

As we sat at the restaurant table having dinner with the owner and his wife, our conversation was centered on Christ.

Looking lovingly at his attractive, vivacious wife, that successful business man said, "I'm thankful for a wife that continued going to church even when I discouraged her. It is because of her life and her faithfulness to her responsibility that I am a Christian today."

His strong Christian character and principles are clearly reflected in his restaurant and employees as well as in other avenues of his life.

Today many fathers must be away from home for extended periods of time. In the father's absence, the mother will assume his responsibilities in the family.

As Dad carries out his place as head of the home - provider, protector and spiritual leader - he is creating in the minds of his family a true picture of God, our Heavenly Father.

> Many young people today cannot comprehend this aspect of God because they do not have this kind of a father in their own home. Dad, you have a BIG responsibility!

Mother
The Heart

of the
Home

The wife and mother in the family has a great responsibility, too, for she is the "heart" of the home. What mother is determines to a large extent what the home and family will be.

MOTHER, as the "heart" of the home, you create the atmosphere of the home.

Think of those mornings when you get up feeling all "cranky and out-of-sorts." On those days *everything* seems to go wrong! Your husband can't find his tie; the toast burns; the baby cries for no reason at all, and Junior just can't tie his shoes or find his boots. About then you wonder why you ever decided that marriage would be fun!

A little 7-year-old asked a visitor to her home, "Do you know what mood my mom's in today?"

Now recall mornings when you have had a good night's sleep and wakened refreshed. You are calm in your own spirit and this calmness is transmitted to the rest of the family. You speak with quiet authority to the children and they respond quietly. You are not upset yourself so you do not upset others.

For many years now a popular women's magazine has had as its slogan, "Never underestimate the power of a woman." How true that is! But it is important to remember that this power can be for good or evil.

One of our American presidents once said, "The hand that rocks the cradle is the hand that rules the world." What a responsibility this places on each mother.

One of the prime requisites for a happy marriage is to remember that you **never** marry a man to reform him. If he has not changed his bad habits before marriage, he will rarely change after! Unless, of course, he is changed by Christ.

So when you are looking for someone with whom you will spend the rest of your life, look for one who has the character traits and qualities that you admire. If they are not evident in the man you date, there is not much likelihood that they will develop just by going through the wedding ceremony!

Having a happy marriage is not so dependent on *finding* the "right" partner as in *being* the "right" partner. Marriage is **not** a 50-50 proposition. Each one must be willing to give 100% of himself/herself into making it a smooth-working partnership.

A few years ago, a well-known minister in the East often presented to the bride and groom two little bear figurines. "These," he would tell the couple, "are named 'bear' and 'forebear.' If you will keep these two as part of your family, your marriage is not likely to end 'on the rocks.'"

REMEMBER WHEN?

Can you remember back to when you were not married?

Remember how you waited for the man in your life to help you with your coat. . .open the door. . .make the dinner engagements? Remember when you snuggled against him in the car?

A middle-aged couple were driving down the highway one day when the woman remarked: "Remember, Honey, how it used to be when we drove anywhere? You really liked it when I was sitting real close to you - and so did I! Now look at the distance between us."

Her husband replied, "Well, I'm still sitting in the same spot behind the wheel. I haven't moved."

REMEMBER how thrilled you were over every gift he gave you, no matter how large or small, how needed or wanted. Always there was that dazzling smile and an extra kiss (or two!) to show your appreciation.

REMEMBER how quickly you came to his defense (whether he needed it or not) if Mom or Dad criticized your "one and only"? Especially if they should happen to point out some of his weaknesses that you had already noticed!

REMEMBER that this man who has become your husband is exactly the same man that you dated. He has the same characteristics, the same qualities you always admired in him; the same temperament. The kind of a husband he becomes depends upon the kind of a wife you are. Your actions and reactions will draw out either the best - or the worst - in him. A young wife in the mid-west had a husband who was not "one in Christ" with her. This often caused conflicts and the young woman was most unhappy. Then one day she asked God for an understanding heart. What a difference this made in her relationship with her husband! Today he is much more ready to listen to the claims of Christ.

NOW YOU ARE MARRIED. No time to wait for the niceties of life. You must jump out of the car the minute it stops to run and find Jane to make arrangements for tomorrow.

Now your husband has more financial responsibilities and does not bring you as many gifts as he once did. But even when he does you sort of take them for granted. Your "thank yous" aren't so spontaneous or enthusiastic now.

One husband was questioned about not bringing home those unexpected gifts any more, or even remembering special days with a gift. His comment was, "There's no fun in giving to an ungrateful person." Do you have a slighting remark to make about what he brings you? Or maybe you take it back the next day!

The Bible teaches us that gratitude is a very important Christian characteristic. When this is a real part of our lives, we will express our thanks to our husbands, our children, our friends and to all who help us, as well as to our Lord.

Remember how you used to dress to attract "his" attention? Those dates were very important times to you for he was a V.I.P. (very important person)! You wanted your hair to be shining and pretty; you wore the outfit you knew would elicit the most compliments from him. In short, you wanted to show him how much you cared by looking your very best for him.

How is it now? Are you saying to your husband, "You are not very important to me anymore." Oh, not in words, perhaps, but by your unkempt look.

How you dress not only gives your husband the "message," but it affects your acts and actions throughout the day. How easy it is to become untidy in our habits when we are untidy in our dress. A well-groomed look gives us confidence.

For months a young husband sat across the breakfast table each morning from an "apparition" with huge curlers in her hair, a worn-out robe and slippers and no make-up. Suddenly one morning he walked over to his wife's chair, picked her up and headed for the front door.

"What are you doing?" she asked. "Where are you taking me?"

"I just wanted the neighbors to see what I have to look at every morning," was his reply.

He never really would have taken her outside, but that was enough to alert that young wife to her appearance each morning.

Of course you won't have on your best dress to prepare breakfast in the morning. But how about getting up in time to comb your hair, put on your make-up and, at least, have on a pretty, clean robe if you don't have time to dress.

In the first few years of her married life, the young bride had delighted in dressing to look attractive to her husband and to others. Later, she grew careless.

Then one day her neighbor noticed that Hilda had begun to take more care in her appearance and commented, "My, you're sure dressing up a lot these days." To which Hilda replied, "My husband has a new secretary."

REMEMBER - the image of you that your husband carries out the door each morning is the one he will compare with those secretaries in his office or the gals on the commuter train. How do you "stack up?" Will he go to work thinking about how wonderful it's going to be to come home to you?

Getting it All

Together

Organization is an important ingredient in a well-run home. That familiar little placard you so often see is a great reminder.

PLAN AHEA
D

Each day needs to be planned in advance, deciding what you wish to accomplish that day. Decide your priorities. Do you need to take something out of the freezer for your evening meal? Must you do some essential shopping that can't wait? Remember, the Bible says we must do everything decently and in order. Planning ahead gives time to accomplish all that must be completed as well as time for other activities.

I had a delightful mother-in-law who was known all over our area as a very fine housekeeper. I wanted to have just as nice a home for my husband as his parents had provided. This meant that I had to learn to organize my time if I wanted a well-run home and still have time for my Christian activities.

Each morning I wakened at 6:00 a.m. to begin my day with God. Thirty minutes was spent reading God's Word so He could speak to me. Then another thirty minutes was spent talking with Him in prayer.

At 7:20, breakfast was on the table and my husband, the two children and I sat down together for breakfast, all of us dressed and ready for the day. Breakfast over, there was time for prayer together before the children took off for school and my husband to his business.

Soon the dishes were done, beds made and I was planning and preparing for our evening meal. On Mondays, the washing was done.

(That was the way my mother-in-law did, you see.) Tuesday was ironing. Friday was for cleaning. And so on. Because I learned to organize my time, there was always time for my Christian activities.

With the many aids the modern homemaker has available, her home can be well-cared-for and still allow her time for some outside interests. It has been proven that it is mentally stimulating and physically refreshing for the wife to be involved in wholesome activities outside her home.

Study groups are available in many areas and home Bible studies such as the Friendship Bible Coffees are the "in" thing all across our continent. These can involve not only the mother, but the father, also. Even teenagers are finding Friendship Bible Chip 'n' Dip exciting!

But a word of warning! In organizing your life, don't organize the Lord right out of it! There is another word that is very important in the life of a Christian. Be "fluid" - not "congealed into a mold" or "set in your ways" so that nothing could change you!

God has mapped out each day of your life. Have you ever consulted Him about your programming? Sometimes He may have some surprises for you! One day He may plan to bring someone across your path that needs to know Him. You can have the privilege of making the introduction IF you are willing to exchange **your** plans for **His**.

I shall always remember the afternoon I was sitting at my desk catching up on my correspondence. The door bell rang and I glanced out the window to see a stranger at the door. I decided not to go to answer the ring. I had planned to use this time for letter writing. Whatever the man was selling, I didn't need or want.

Then the Spirit of God spoke to me. Oh, not in an audible voice, of course; but I heard Him. "How did you pray this morning? Could this be a person who needs to know about Me?"

The doorbell rang again. This time I got up from my desk and walked to the door. I was remembering the motto hanging on the wall in full view of anyone standing at our door. It read:

Only one life;
  'Twill soon be passed.
Only what's done for Christ
  Will last.

"Need anything sharpened today, Lady? Any knives, scissors. . .?"

I didn't know whether anything needed to be sharpened or not, but I said, "Yes, you can sharpen the lawn mower. Just go around to the back and you can get it from the basement."

Seated in the shade of the fig tree, the man began to work on the mower. I slipped back into the house and brought him something cold to drink. After that it was easy to carry on a conversation while he worked.

Soon we began to talk about God. With a look almost of relief, that man said, "Lady, I rode into this city this morning 'on the rails.' As we came into town I said, 'O God, if there be a God, have somebody talk with me about You today!'"

"Lady," he continued, "I've been all up and down 9th Street and this far along 10th Street and you are the first person who has talked with me about God."

I felt so badly when I heard that, for I knew several Christian families who lived in that area who could have talked with him about God - but didn't.

Recognizing that this man was longing to know God, I invited him to have dinner with us that evening so he could meet my husband. He accepted the invitation gladly and a few minutes before 5:30 that evening was back at our door neatly groomed.

That night my husband introduced that young Texan to Jesus Christ. He was one of the last people my husband ever witnessed to, for in just a few weeks my husband met with a terrible accident and went to be with his Lord. What if I had been unwilling to change my plans!

What is the top priority in your life? Are you willing to allow God to change your plans so that He can accomplish His purpose through you? Can you "keep your cool" even when you are not able to carry out everything you had planned for that day?

That Man
in Your
Life

Today men are living under greater pressures than, perhaps, any other time in history. The fast tempo of our age demands speed in everything. The tension just in getting to work every day is nerve-wracking!

Competition in both the business and professional world is keen. Expanding business calls for much travel. Plane schedules must be met. Production must be increased to take care of rising costs. Laws are constantly changing so that keeping up with them adds more pressure. A man has to "produce" or some-one else will take his place. Even his seniority seems to count for little these days, and a position of responsibility does not guarantee that he will not be replaced.

Add to this the pressures of his family responsibilities: providing a good, warm home for his family - air conditioned in the summer! Supplying food and clothing. Providing for medical and dental care; education; recreation and social needs.

Surely a man needs a "helpmeet" - one who stands with him, is understanding and loving, who has discernment to know how to meet his needs.

In a recent telephone conversation, a business executive commented, "Do you know what's going to happen this year?"

You might have thought of many answers to that question. But the thought uppermost in his mind was the fact that this year he would turn 50!

"What's so bad about that?" you ask.

In many companies today the trend is to keep *young* men in places of responsibility. When a man reaches 50 he is considered almost "over the hill." So here is another pressure point. "How long will the company keep me" is a thought that is constantly with him.

There are many ways that you, as the "heart" of the home and his wife, can be a real help to your husband.

First of all, **LOVE HIM**. Not a "gushy," maudlin feeling that demands his attention, but a deep, quiet affection that is expressed in all your attitudes and actions.

APPRECIATE HIM. Your husband wants you to appreciate him and his accomplishments. After all, he is doing all this for you. So you don't understand why it's such a "big deal" that he had lunch with Mr. Smith today. But he's excited about it, so you can show some enthusiasm, too. Maybe your husband isn't "Mr. Handi-man" around the house, but when he puts up those shelves in the basement or repairs the children's toys, do you show him your appreciation? Admire and build-up your husband to him and to others.

COMPLIMENT HIM. Compliment your husband as often as you can. Remember all those great qualities of his you talked about and admired before you were married? They are still there! They just need you to bring them out. Concentrate on his good points and minimize the others, even in your own thinking. Remember, the Bible says *love covers*.

Here's how one wife expressed her appreciation:

43

Dear Verne,

Happy Birthday, Darling, to the one and only special person in my life. How thankful I am that the Lord saw fit to bring us together.

Just wanted to thank you for the leadership, spiritually and physically, you give in our home; for your wonderful care and concern through the years. I really appreciate and enjoy being a wife, mother and homemaker.

Your decision early in our marriage for me not to work outside the home has meant much, too. Your trust and confidence in relation to money - I never have to beg for money.

Thank you for being neat about yourself in appearance and hanging up your clothes. Thank you for all the many little chores and fix-it jobs you do continually, and however difficult, you always have a solution. Nothing seems too difficult a task for you.

Most of all, for your love and warmth, in spite of my failures, I thank you. I'm proud to call you my husband.

May your day be filled with blessing which you deserve.

Lovingly,

NEVER, NEVER, NEVER, NEVER criticize your husband or "put him down" before others. Of course, there will be times when you can't agree wholeheartedly with him, but the Bible says, *"Speaking the truth in love."* [15] Tact is just as important in your marriage as it is in settling world affairs.

Some time ago, a guest was visiting in a home where the wife was a Christian but her husband had not yet committed his life to Christ. At one point in the conversation there was a discussion about some church meetings the wife had just attended. As she spoke of the inspiration she had received, the wife said to her husband, "But next time I don't want to go unless you go with me."

The guest was delighted, until he heard the wife's next comment. "I don't need it, but you do!"

Although the guest hastened to change the subject, the damage had been done. There would be no desire on the part of that husband to attend any meetings with her.

ENCOURAGE HIM. Be an "encourager" for your husband. Have confidence in what he does and let him know that you do. There are so many things to discourage him. In describing a good wife, the Bible says, *"She will comfort, encourage and do him* [her husband] *only good as long as there is life within her."* [16] Do you know how to sympathize with him when he makes a mistake? Show him that you do understand how he feels, and then encourage him to try again. Your confidence in him will give him confidence in himself.

BE SENSITIVE TO YOUR HUSBAND'S MOODS. When he is wrestling with a weighty decision or feeling low because sales or stocks are down, this is *not* the time to begin talking about that darling coat you saw with the mink collar. Nor about sending the children to private schools! Instead, how about a good dinner with his favorite dessert and time to sit and "toast your toes" by the fireplace.

After a busy day at the office, a man looks forward to coming home for some peace and quiet. Is yours that kind of a home? When you know he has had an especially hectic day - or even if he hasn't - do you meet him at the door with all your own frustrations and problems? Or have you learned the great value of a quiet spirit every day? Save those problems to talk over when the children are in bed and both of you are more relaxed.

I remember evenings in my own home when my husband would sit down and pick up the newspaper. Sometimes I would begin a conversation only to have him say, "Honey, I have been talking to people all day. Do you mind if I don't talk tonight? Just having you here in the room with me is all I want."

BE CONSIDERATE. A friend once remarked, "There are two kinds of people - owls and chickens - and she's both of them!" She was referring to the fact that her friend wakes up "bright-eyed and bushy-tailed" early each morning and is still "going strong" late into the night. But few people are like that! So when an "owl" and a "chicken" marry, there has to be plenty of consideration on the part of each of them.

NEVER, NEVER GO TO BED ANGRY WITH EACH OTHER. The Bible says, *"Let not the sun go down upon your wrath."* [17] Talk it out. . .forgive. . .and **forget!** Don't be like the couple who made a pact that they would never go to sleep angry with each other. Once they didn't sleep for four days!

The writer of the book of HEBREWS in the Bible wisely wrote: *"Be careful that none of you fails to respond to the grace which God gives, for if he does, there can very easily spring up in him a bitter spirit which is not only bad in itself but can also poison the lives of many others."* [18]

It takes two to make a quarrel, you know; but one can stop it. Are you willing to say, "I was wrong; will you forgive me?"

47

The purpose of forgiveness is to make things right between you and to bring back peace and harmony into your relationship. Don't try to project the blame on someone else; don't go all through the argument again; don't qualify your request for forgiveness. Simply admit you were wrong and ask forgiveness. Or, if the other person is wrong, be willing to forgive and **forget**.

The Bible says, *"Be kind to one another; be understanding. Be as ready to forgive others as God for Christ's sake has forgiven you."*[19] How does God forgive? He forgives and forgets. He says, *"And their sins and iniquities will I remember no more."* [20] Can you learn to forgive and forget?

When you have asked the other person's forgiveness, or assured him of yours, then ask God to forgive you, also. Remember, when Jesus was teaching His disciples, He said, ". . . *if you forgive other people their failures, your Heavenly Father will also forgive you."* [21]

Remember our story about the bride who wanted to go to the shore in August, but her husband's company assigned his vacation in July? After their discussion, hubby considered that a closed subject. There was no way of changing his vacation, so they would just plan that way.

But the little wife didn't forget so easily. All evening she kept thinking about the family being at the shore without her. It just wasn't fair! They had a right to vacation in August if they wanted! That night she tossed and turned and could not sleep.

Morning found her cranky and out-of-sorts. A coffee break with her neighbor gave her opportunity to enlarge on the subject and get some sympathy from her friend. All day it grew bigger and bigger in her mind.

By the time hubby arrived home for dinner that evening, the explosion came! Angry words, tears, accusations ("You don't really love me!") - and a bewildered husband. Busy at the office all day, he had long since forgotten the incident of yesterday. All the restlessness, the bitterness, the angry words could have been avoided if the wife had just committed this to the Lord. He would have given her peace of mind and contentment. . .and she wouldn't have had that acid indigestion brought on by her frustration!

Because

You Love Him

BE A GOOD LISTENER. Be truly interested in what your husband is interested in and in those things he wants to share with you. So you don't know a goal post from second base. Read the sports page anyhow, every now and then, and be familiar with at least some of the names he mentions. Ask some intelligent questions and show him that you really do want to understand something about the sports he enjoys.

And if you can't enjoy his interests, at least let him enjoy them!

BE HIS REAL CONFIDANTE. Are you able to keep your husband's confidences? Can you imagine how a husband felt when his wife mentioned casually to him, "By the way, I was telling Jean, next door, what you told me about the problem you were having with that new man in the office. She said he is a close friend of theirs and her husband will talk with him about it." Your husband needs to be able to talk with you about anything, knowing that it will never go any further - not even to your closest and best friend.

TRY TO SEE THINGS FROM HIS POINT OF VIEW. Granted, men think with their heads and women with their hearts, but have you tried putting yourself in his place? After being at home all day, of course you would "love to go out to eat." But remember that he has been "bucking traffic" and is tired of pushing himself to meet the many demands of the day. He would like to come home and "collapse" for a while. Remember, the Bible says **love gives**. [22]

BE INTERESTING TO COME HOME TO. Every day isn't going to go exactly as you had planned it. But planning does help! Why not plan to read something-new-to-you while you eat your lunch or stop for a quick coffee

52

break. Find interesting things that could "spark up" the dinner table conversation. Keep a good book handy that will give you short, interesting bits of information.

For example, try **The Birds and the Bees** by John Jess. It gives such fascinating information such as: All snow flakes are six-sided and all sides are the same length. There are 96 varieties of snow flakes in the Artic Circle. You might even mention that the word "snow" appears 24 times in the Bible!

Can't you just see Junior's eyes widen in amazement when you comment, "Did you know that birds are the fastest creatures on our planet? A falcon can dive on its prey at speeds up to 180 miles per hour." The children (and maybe even your husband) will be amazed to know that a bird of prey has a third eyelid which is drawn back and forth across the eyeball like a windshield wiper to keep the eyeball free of dust and other irritants.

Or you might try these interesting facts about the human heart. This most interesting "machine" is about the size of one's fist and weighs somewhat more than half a pound. The volume of blood pumped by the heart in one year is about 650,000 gallons, or enough to fill more than 81 tank cars of 8,000 gallons each! The blood circulates through about 12,000 miles of bloodways, or the approximate distance from New York to Hong Kong by way of the Panama Canal!

Such "conversation pieces" not only create interesting table conversation, but may create an interest in a child's mind that will set him studying more about that subject.

Another fascinating mealtime pastime is learning a new word - how to spell it, how to use it.

COMMUNICATE WITH YOUR HUSBAND. Good communication is essential to a happy marriage. This does not mean, necessarily, just conversation. If you and your husband are "on the same wave length," just a look or a smile can communicate volumes!

But there are things that need to be talked about, too. Jimmy has been coming home from school with some strange ideas. Should we—or can we afford to send the children to Christian school? What about plans for vacation? Financial matters need to be discussed. Should we get the house painted this year or wait until next spring? You felt your husband was too hard on Jane when she came in late. These are things that **do** need to be talked about - but at the right time and in the right spirit.

Maybe there is some fear, some uncertainty, some problem going over and over in your mind. Keeping it to yourself and just mulling it over enlarges it all out of proportion. Confide in your husband and let his calm, clear thinking put it back into the right perspective.

54

FINANCES. This can be a big point of contention if not handled properly. There should be a real agreement between husband and wife as to how the money is to be spent.

In all probability, the two of you have more or less outlined your over-all budget. Perhaps when you were single you didn't operate on a budget. You just spent what you earned as you decided. But now there are two people to be considered.

How well I remember the time, as a young bride, when I assured my husband I'd be real happy to take over paying the bills. Everything went along fine and I was proudly showing my husband, at the end of the month, how every bill was paid and I had used just the amount we had planned. Then my husband said, "What about the house payment?" I'd forgotten about that!

Have you learned to live within your budget? That will save a lot of friction! You would love to have a new dress. . .but Timmy needs new shoes. Do you pout and fuss, or do you show your maturity by using your ingenuity to make one of your old dresses look like new?

"OKAY! LET'S. . ." Have you ever analyzed how you respond to your husband's suggestions? Do you find that more and more you are saying, "I'd rather not go there tonight" or "Must we invite them over?"

Think how you would have responded be-

55

fore you were married. "Great! I'd love to.." no matter what it was! Why not try responding positively to your husband's suggestions whenever possible, and being gracious when you can't. Your answer doesn't always have to be "yes" but it can be a *gracious* "no."

In a recent newspaper column in the Kansas City Times, Ann Landers gave these

Rules for a Happy Married Life

1. Never both be angry at once.

2. Never yell at each other unless the house is on fire.

3. Yield to the wishes of the other as an exercise in self-discipline if you can't think of a better reason.

4. If you have a choice between making yourself look good or your mate - choose your mate.

5. If you have any criticism, make it lovingly.

6. Never bring up a mistake of the past.

7. Neglect the whole world rather than each other.

8. Never let the day end without saying at least one complimentary thing to your life's partner.

9. Never meet without an affectionate welcome.

10. Never go to bed mad.

11. When you've made a mistake, talk it out and ask for forgiveness.

12. Remember, it takes two to make an argument. The one who is wrong is the one who will be doing most of the talking.

The Feminine You

Femininity is that magnificent but elusive quality that every young girl yearns to develop and every older woman longs to keep. It is that quality in a woman which makes her different from a man - his counterpart, his booster, his admirer as God intended her to be.

A man thinks with his head; a woman with her heart. God created us different for a purpose.

To man, God gave the strong drives and abilities that make him the provider, the builder, the financier.

To woman, God gave tenderness, empathy, creativity, supple strength and all the qualities that enable her to find fulfillment in creating beauty and comfort in the home. Soothing a small child's hurts. **Creating an atmosphere of peace and harmony.** Training the children for a life of purpose and achievement. Supplying the love, understanding and responsiveness that builds up and encourages her husband. This is the feminine you.

How often have you decided, "I'll take just a minute to call Pat" only to have it take 45 minutes? Not that there was any special news, but one thing led to another and before you knew it, most of an hour was gone!

The telephone, properly used, is a wonderful invention. But there are dangers involved. Who can ever assess the amount of gossip that has travelled over telephone wires ending in hurt feelings, broken friendships, untrue accusations, even ruined lives. It's so easy, when you are "just talking" to pass on some little rumor that ruins a reputation.

The Bible says, ". . .*the human tongue is physically small, but what tremendous effects it can boast of! A whole forest can be set a-*

blaze by a tiny spark of fire and the tongue is as dangerous as any fire. . ." [23]

Long telephone conversations will undo all your planning. "My neighbor called and talked to me for an hour! After that I just could not get back on schedule. She does that all the time." Because of the phone call, you are late picking up the children at school. . .which makes you late with your shopping. . .which makes you late with dinner. . .which makes your husband late for that important meeting! And everyone is under tension!

We **do** want to be friendly with our neighbors as this **is** part of our witness for Christ. But you must be sensitive to recognize when you are able to minister to them and when it is just a case of "killing time." Keep your priorities straight! Time is too valuable to "kill." You can always say, "I just love talking with you, Jean, but you know how we limit our teenagers on the phone. Guess I'd better stick to that rule myself!"

Whatever phoning you are going to do, do it during the day and not all evening while your husband sits alone, or gets tired of the phone interrupting his conversation with you.

Remember when you were dating? You saved your evenings just for him!

The husband-wife relationship is more important than any other in the home. Keep it strong, tender, kind and good.

A wise person once wrote: "Preserve sacredly the privacies of your own house, your married state and your heart. Let no father or mother or sister or brother ever presume to come between you or share the joys or sorrows that belong to you two alone. With mutual help, build your quiet world, allowing your dearest earthly friend to be the confidante of naught that concerns your domestic peace. Let moments of alienation, if they occur, be healed at once. **Never,** no **never** speak of it outside; but to each other confess and all will come out right. Renew and renew your vow. It will do you good; and thereby your minds will grow together contented in that love which is stronger than death, and you will be truly one."

About now, some of you are saying, "But you don't know my husband!"

Let me tell you about two of our friends. When they were married, neither of them had a personal relationship with Jesus Christ. Through the ministry of the Village Missionary in their community, the wife accepted Christ as her Saviour. She was excited and wanted her husband to have this same new joy she had. But he did not respond to her enthusiasm.

In fact, he seemed to become antagonistic. At first, this made her angry, until she realized that, as a Christian, she no longer had any "right" to be angry. So she prayed and asked God to help her to be the kind of a witness for Him that would cause her husband to desire what she had.

A few nights later, instead of coming home for dinner at the usual time, her husband came in several hours later, with no explanation. Out came the food, and a good dinner was served in a pleasant atmosphere with friendly conversation.

Time passed. Another night a promise to be home at 6:30 for dinner with guests was not kept. Instead, it was midnight before he arrived. Again the wife got up and prepared him something to eat just as if this were the usual procedure.

Then came the night when he was out until the wee hours of the morning. Later, when telling us this story, the husband said, "I wanted to really test her to see if what she had was real. It sure was hard to find any place to spend so many hours in our little town for they fold up the sidewalks at 9 o'clock!" So he finally went to sleep in the car, and returned home about 3:00 a.m.

Breakfast time brought never a word of recrimination from the wife. She told him she had been real concerned about him and hoped he wouldn't be too tired at school.

It was then that high school coach broke down. He told his wife that he wanted whatever it was she had that made her so easy to get along with. Whatever it was had drastically changed her life.

How thrilled that dear wife was to be able to share with her husband the wonderful story of Christ's redeeming love for him. Right there he received Christ as his own personal Saviour.

Perhaps this is all best summed up in the words of the great Apostle Paul who wrote:

> *"LOVE knows no limit to its endurance,*
> *no end to its trust,*
> *no fading of its hope;*
> *it can outlast anything.*
> *It is, in fact, the one thing that still stands*
> *when all else has fallen."* [24]

Those Bundles of Joy

As part of His magnificent plan, God gave man the great gift of love. Two people who love each other are united in holy marriage. They separate themselves from everyone else and keep themselves for each other. From this beautiful union God gives the tiny baby.

Babies are living proof that "the twain shall be one flesh." How often we exclaim, "The little one has eyes just like his mother" . . .or "hair just like her daddy." Even the parents' actions are passed on to the child - the way he walks; his manner of speech; even his disposition!

With father as the head of the family and mother as the heart, both parents have a grave responsibility for the spiritual as well as the physical upbringing of the children God gives to them.

The Bible says, *"My son, hear the instruction of thy father, and forsake not the law of thy mother ."* 25

It is wise for the mother to remember that children are never to take the place of her husband in her life. His is the primary position; together they carry the responsibility of the children.

Because the mother spends so many hours each day with the children, she has a great opportunity to make an impact on their lives. What the children see in their home and in the lives of their parents will affect the kind of homes they will establish in the future. In writing to Timothy, the Apostle Paul said, *"I often think of that genuine faith of yours - a faith that first appeared in your grandmother Lois, then in Eunice, your mother, and is now, I am convinced, in you as well."* 26

LOVE THEM

A career military officer was sharing the

things in his parents' lives that had molded his life. "One of the outstanding things I remember," he said, "was their love for the Lord Jesus which they expressed by their love for each other."

Even between Christian parents, differences of opinion may arise, but should be taken care of when you two are alone. Quarreling and fussing before the children gives them a real sense of insecurity. Christian parents have the asset of prayer through which to settle these differences.

Perhaps you are a Christian mother with a non-Christian husband. Differences of opinion concerning the children are not always so easily resolved in your home since you cannot resort to prayer **together**. However, **you** can spend some time each day in prayer for each of your children.

Susannah Wesley, who lived many years ago, was the mother of 19 children. Needless to say, there was little time or place where she could be alone to pray. But when the children saw Mother sitting in her rocker with her apron thrown over her head, they knew she was talking with God, and no one disturbed her.

One by one, Susannah brought each of her children to God in prayer each day, and spent one hour each week with each of them alone. In these intervening years, tens of thousands of people have become Christians through the preaching and singing of John and Charles Wesley and the great ministry they founded.

Do you love your children?

DISCIPLINE THEM

Another factor in the life of this Marine officer was the loving discipline he received at home. He remembers that he did not enjoy it at the time, but now he appreciates what his parents did.

The Bible says, *"Train up a child in the way he should go: and when he is old, he will not depart from it."* [27]

Disciplining a child means more than just spanking him when he misbehaves. The word "discipline" comes from the same root word as "disciple." A disciple is one who learns through association with the teacher, not only from the words spoken, but from the life lived before him.

How true this is of our children! If Dad is "fudging" on his income tax, can he be surprised when son cheats at school? When Mother's telephone conversations include all the latest gossip, can we say anything about daughter when she carries tales and stirs up trouble?

What kind of a housekeeper will your daughter be if she follows your example? Or, perhaps, you do keep the house in order, but have to keep the doors into the children's rooms closed because they look like a "disaster area."

Does your daughter leave her clothes right where she steps out of them? Does son get away each day without putting away his things? Does the bathroom look like a tornado swept through it by the time they all leave for school?

Teaching children to care for their clothes, their toys, their rooms must start at a very early age. Make it a game for 2-year-old Jimmy to put his toys away when he has finished playing. Then when he is eight and comes in from playing ball, it will be easier for him to remember not to throw his bat on the floor and leave his ball and glove on the stairs! But it takes constant, consistent, loving, imaginative training on the part of the parents to achieve this.

If we expect teenage Judy to have a room in which her blue jeans are hung in the closet and her bed is made, we must begin when Judy is a tiny tot to train her how to take care of her things. This is one way of teaching her the value of money.

CONSISTENT TRAINING

Being consistent with children is a major factor in their training. Perhaps you have said, "Jimmy, don't go outside in that rain or I'll spank you." But, like most children, Jimmy decides to test you to see if you really mean it. So out he goes.

By this time you are busy doing something else - maybe even talking on the phone - and don't bother to follow through on your statement. Jimmy now knows that he can get away with things and your words will have little or no meaning to him.

If children are not taught to obey their **parents,** they often find it difficult to obey **God.** If their rebellion is not curbed early in life, they will continue to rebel against all authority. Children must have their will broken, but not their spirit.

Tommy, the youngest of three children, was still too young to go to school when a visitor came to their home. As his mother talked with the visitor in the living room, Tommy stood in the kitchen and called, "Mommy, Mommy, come here." Again, "Mommy, I want a drink of water." All during the brief visit, Tommy was seeking and getting his mother's attention. Constantly, Mother was "on the run" for Tommy.

The dinner hour in the evening was no better. What food Tommy didn't want went on the floor, and there were constant calls for something different. The two older children were well-behaved and a pleasure to have at the table.

Later that evening, when it seemed to come

spontaneously, the visitor commented: "Do you know that you are not being fair to Tommy? If he is allowed to continue to have his own way and disobey, no one will want him around. It really isn't fair to him to bring him up this way."

Telling someone else how to rear their children is certainly a dangerous subject! But that night it must have been done under the guidance of the Holy Spirit. Some three weeks later, the mother said to that visitor, "Remember our conversation about Tommy when you were at our home? At first, I thought, 'Why should she be telling me how to rear my child?' But then I realized that you had spoken in love, and I didn't resent it."

"You see," the mother continued, "we read a book which said that we should never discipline a child in front of others. It didn't take Tommy long to learn how this worked and to take advantage of it. Although he is normally a sweet, obedient child when we are alone, as soon as company comes, he begins to misbehave because he knows he won't get spanked while company is here. When they are gone, it is too late or we forget.

"But since my conversation with you, my husband and I have realized that we can no longer follow that plan. Now we discipline him when he needs it, and **our whole family is happier!**"

Disciplining children does not mean that

you are continually "yelling" at them! Children are thankful for boundaries and a voice of authority. Teenagers have told how grateful they were to be able to say, "Oh, Mom won't let me go" so they could blame the parent instead of having to make the decision themselves.

The well-known radio preacher, Ben Haden, tells of a 14-year-old girl who received a phone call one day and squealed with delight. Then came her comment, "Just a minute; I'll have to ask Mom and Dad."

"Mom! Dad! Can I go to the Drive-In with Sammy? He just asked me!"

Simultaneously, Mom and Dad said "no."

Linda burst out crying and continued to sob over the phone as she tried to explain to Sammy that her parents had said no. A little later she appeared in the room again and said, "Thanks. Thanks, Mom and Dad, for saying no."

The Drive-In was an experience Linda didn't know how to cope with and it was a real relief to her not to have to face it.

One little girl grew up thinking her parents didn't love her because they never spanked her! We're not sure she knew it, but that is what the Bible says: *". . .whom the Lord loveth, He chasteneth. . .No true son ever grows up uncorrected by his father...After all, when we were children we had fathers who corrected us, and we respected them for it."* [28]

72

As Christian parents, when disciplining, it is important that you let your child know that although you do not like the wrong thing he does, you still love him. Through this he will learn the same truth about God. The Bible says, *"He who spares his rod hates his son, but he who loves him disciplines him diligently."* 29

Remember, you have those precious children for only a few short years, at best, to prepare them for the years ahead. God has given you, the parents, the responsibility of training them; of teaching them self-discipline; of helping to shape the habits which will affect their entire lives and even their eternal destiny.

SPIRITUAL TRAINING

Having a family time together is really important for proper spiritual training. But it is important, also, to avoid having this time become just a routine through which the family goes regularly, without any meaning. Have variety in your devotional time. Consider the ages of the children when choosing the material to be used in addition to the Bible. As the children get older, let them participate by reading or by answering questions as well as in praying.

Our Marine Lieutenant friend told of the plan his father had for conducting family devotions. After father read the Bible passage and, perhaps, a short devotional message, the youngest child would ask a question about it of the next older child. He, in turn, asked a question of the next older, and so on. This insured everyone paying attention and had the added advantage of having the children actively involved.

While visiting in another home, seated at the dinner table, we were delighted to hear the father begin their time of devotion by asking each child to repeat a Bible verse. Various ones responded. Then the youngest, 8-year-old Nancy, eyes sparkling, said, "I know one" and proceeded to repeat the entire first Psalm!

What a heritage these children have with the Word of God tucked away in their minds and hearts!

As soon as the children can read with understanding, they should be encouraged to have their own "quiet time" each day. Many easily-read devotional books for children are available. Even five minutes a day could develop a life-long pattern.

Little Lucy was an avid reader and at the age of 11 or 12 was already reading some of the Dickens' novels she found on the shelf, along with many of the old classics.

Seeing her daughter's great interest, Lucy's mother sat down with her one day and gave her a Bible to read. She opened the pages in the back and explained the schedule given there. By following this schedule in reading so many chapters each morning and night, she could read the Bible through in one year.

"Don't you think this would be good to do?" Mother asked. "Suppose I call you ten minutes earlier each morning so you can read the chapters and then pray before you come down for breakfast."

This became a real habit with little Lucy.

It was only a short time later that Lucy's mother went to be with the Lord and Lucy became the mother to her sisters and brothers. But her program of Bible reading continued. Today, Lucy is not only a real student of the Word of God, but a full-time missionary in America and the author of our Friendship Bible Coffees lessons!

The real goal of a family devotional time is to bring your children to the point of accepting Christ personally and then to nurture them in their spiritual growth. One of the greatest joys of a parent is the privilege of introducing his own children to Christ.

Children Are People

BE AN ENCOURAGER

Little Roland had been so excited for days! He had brought a note from his teacher saying he would need fifty cents to buy some supplies. He talked and talked about this wonderful surprise he would be bringing home to Mother. She was excited, too.

Roland worked and worked on his project. The great day came - he could take it home! But, alas, things at home had changed. Mother was no longer there. She had gone to be with the Lord.

Roland handed the picture to his father rather hesitantly. After one quick glance, his father said, "Is this what I spent my money on? What's that supposed to be? It doesn't look like anything to me."

The little boy was deeply hurt. Oh, how he needed Mother. She would have said, "Did you really do this yourself? Isn't it lovely! You are doing so well in your work and Mother surely appreciates your making this for her."

Because of his father's reaction, Roland cried and cried and could not be consoled. And father could not understand.

Every child needs encouragement. Challenge him to do his best, but remember, don't expect too much of him. Compliment him as often as you honestly can without causing him to be "puffed up."

No doubt you have heard the fable of the Wind and the Sun as they disputed who was the strongest. They finally decided to settle the argument by seeing who could get a man who was walking down the street to take off his coat.

Wind blew and blew, but the stronger he blew, the closer the man wrapped his coat around him.

Then Sun began in his gentle way to shine on the man. Warmer and warmer he shone and in almost no time at all off came the coat.

While all kinds of interpretations might be made of this story, it certainly can serve to remind us that gentleness is often more effective than strength. How often praise achieves much better results than criticism! Somehow, most of us seem to react negatively to criticism and a spirit of rebellion results.

King David of old once wrote, *". . .thy gentleness hath made me great."* [30]

WE DO IT THIS WAY

You have heard, as I have, that plaintive whine, "But Susie's mother said she could go, so why can't I?" Or, "But everybody's doing it!"

Any orderly society has to have rules and the family unit is no exception. Father and mother should work together to set up the standards and rules they want for their family and both should be careful to carry these out in their training and discipline.

Some families, when the children get a little older, like to have a "family council time" when the entire family has a part in discussing plans, helping to set limits, etc. This is another avenue of training.

But remember, Dad and Mom, you are still

the ones God holds responsible. You are the voice of authority and, as parents, you should never abdicate this authority to the children until they have become adults and are responsible for their own conduct.

A popular pastime for children and young people these days is staying overnight with friends. This is a custom which we feel should not be encouraged as a regular habit, but should be enjoyed only on special occasions. It has been proven best that, at night time, children should be with their parents, in their own beds, following the schedule the parents have for them.

You may be very selective about what your children see and hear, but how do you know what they are doing when they are at Billy's house? Out from under parental restraint, Bobby's imagination can lead him to assure his friend's mother that it's OK to stay up later; he often does at home! Or to see certain programs on TV. Or. . .a thousand and one things!

A FEW DON'TS

DON'T VENT YOUR ANGER ON THE CHILDREN. Of course it gets on your nerves when Kent continually slams the door after you have told him not to a dozen times! Yes, naturally you are upset when Nancy crawls up on the table and knocks down your favorite Belleek pitcher. The children do need to be

80

disciplined when they do wrong in order to understand why they are being punished. But wait until that first flash of anger has cooled down. Then administer the punishment. When you are in that state of mind you could do irreparable harm to your child.

DON'T COMPARE YOUR CHILDREN. Each child God gives you is an individual with his own personality, his own abilities, talents and limitations. Comparisons are seldom appreciated, and are especially difficult for children. "John always made an A in science; how come you only made a C?" "Mary, why don't you pick up your feet. You are as clumsy as your father!" Compliment, encourage, challenge. . .but **don't compare!**

DON'T TRY TO MAKE THEM INTO YOUR MOLD. You always wanted to play the piano but could never take lessons. So Jane **must** have them. It makes no difference that Jane can't even carry a tune and has no interest in music. She **must** take piano.

The day Jim, Jr. was born you were so excited! Here was the boy to follow in his doctor-father's footsteps. So all his training is pointed in that direction. But secretly, Jim, Jr. really would like to be an engineer. . .or a mechanic. . .or a policeman! Have you ever given him an opportunity to express himself, or is his future just a foregone conclusion?

81

Why not just challenge him to use all his potentialities to the fullest and then pray that the Lord will lead him where He wants him.

YOU'RE BEING WATCHED! During the night the snow had fallen and the family wakened to a beautiful white world. No one had walked on the new-fallen snow until Dad went off to work leaving his imprints so clear.

Donnie was excited and could hardly wait to wiggle into his snow suit, get his boots and get out in that lovely wet "stuff." Mommy opened the door, then watched as little Donnie started down the steps. Almost instantly she noticed that Donnie was trying, oh, so hard, to walk in Daddy's footsteps!

Where would it lead your son or daughter if, figuratively speaking, they followed in their parents' footsteps!

Remember, your children are watching you. They are learning what your standards in life are. . .and how you keep them! Do you talk to them about being honest. . .then tell a "little white lie" now and then? Do you insist they go to church each week while you stay at home? Is your philosophy, "Don't do as I do; just do as I say."

Your children are watching your attitudes, your actions. . .and your reactions! We can learn to control our actions, but reactions cannot be controlled. When a glass is tipped, what is inside comes out. If milk, then that white liquid will spread across the table. If something else, then that's what comes out.

So it is in our lives. We may work hard at keeping the bitterness or discontent or negativism under control, but when the unexpected comes, then what is your reaction?

As a Christian, you have the privilege of bringing all your hurts, those thoughts that are not what they should be, all your discontent to Christ. Ask His forgiveness and allow Him to fill you with His love. Then your reactions will be under His control.

Yes, it takes lots of work and discipline and prayer to bring up a family in the nurture and admonition of the Lord, but one letter like the following makes it "worth it all."

Dear Mom,

When God instructed children to "Honor thy father and thy mother" He made it easy for me. You are much loved and have earned my love and respect which I freely give.

I'm very proud of you and feel honored to have a mother like you. I only hope my children can feel somewhat the same toward me.

I love you,

CAUSES OF
INSECURITY IN CHILDREN

Children reflect in their feelings of security or insecurity the kind of home in which they are reared. Outstanding causes of insecurity include:

Lack of love

Rejection - implied or inferred

Emphasis on failures - ridiculing, blaming, nagging, criticizing

Pampering

Over-protection

Lack of honesty and fairness

Tension in the home due to quarreling between parents; divided loyalties, conflict, indecision

Parents' exchange of roles:
Mother dominant
Father doesn't take definite stand

ESSENTIALS TO
A FEELING OF SECURITY
IN CHILDREN

Love

Acceptance - verbal expression of
approval, appreciation

Confidence, trust, encouragement

Freedom to grow up

Opportunity to contribute ideas
and opinions

The privilege of making suggestions

Correction when necessary

Fairness, honesty

Harmony in the home - mutual love,
loyalty, respect

Parents fulfill proper roles.

The ultimate security for any child is found
in his right relationship to God who made him.

Families

Grow

Together With

Love

It has always been my habit to awaken early in the morning. And so it is that when I am visiting in a home I often hear the early morning sounds of the family beginning the day.

First, there is the sound of son's alarm clock. It is turned off and things are quiet for a while. But, at last, I hear the sound of feet "hitting the deck" and soon the refrigerator door creaks. In my mind's eye I can see that tall, lanky teenager take out the milk for some cold cereal which he eats hurriedly, perhaps with a piece of toast, and he's off for the day. Mom hasn't gotten up yet and there's no one to fix him some good hot cakes with syrup or a couple of fried eggs. . .and no one to talk to.

Just about that time the shower which I've heard in daughter's room is silenced and once again I hear the sound of the refrigerator door. This time it's going to be instant breakfast. I hear muffled voices and imagine Mom saying, "Don't you want something besides that cold milk?" But daughter reminds Mom that she's on a diet and doesn't have time for anything else anyhow. And it isn't long before the door closes behind her, too.

Have you ever thought about the difference it would make if Mom were the first one up each day? How much nicer for son to walk into the kitchen to find the table set, Mom looking "neat" and the delightful aroma of hot cakes coming from the skillet. With no one else around, Mom has time to sit across the table and talk a bit. Before long, the conversation turns to what happened the night before, or about the possibility of making the first string team, or where to apply for college entrance.

Then one day, as he leaves, he plants a little

"peck" on your forehead with a "Thanks, Mom." Many a confidence will you get in this way that you would get at no other time. And how great for son to hear you say, "I'll be praying for you" to start his day. Or for daughter to be able to say, "Mom, we're having a test in chemistry today. Could you remember to pray?"

Another "key" time for Mom to be on hand is when that door bursts open after school and you hear, "Anything to eat, Mom?" All the news comes tumbling out as they land in the kitchen. You learn about that little quarrel with Johnny ("Well, he hit me first."), or the honor of being first in class, or the disappointment of not winning a place on the team or a part in the play. What an opportunity to give guidance and encouragement! As the "heart" of the home, be sure to make this one of your priorities.

Keep the lines of communication open with your young people. It's important. It takes work. But it's worth it! We can't command their confidences, but we can win them. Being available at strategic moments is one way. Being interested in what they are doing is another.

LOOKS MAKE THE DIFFERENCE! Time had gotten away that morning and the weather was a bit cool, so Mom offered to drive her young son to school. He quickly accepted the offer and everything was fine until they arrived within a block of the building.

"Why don't you drop me off right here, Mom," David remarked. "I can walk the rest of the way and you can go on up this street."

Mom assured him she really didn't mind taking him all the way, but he insisted he would get out right there.

Bewildered, Mom went on home and then forgot the incident. That is, she forgot it until the next time she drove David to school. This time he said, "Why don't you drop me off right over there by my buddies, Mom."

All that day Mom pondered over the difference. When a convenient opportunity arose, she asked David about it.

"Why was it you wanted me to drop you off a block from school the other day, but yesterday you asked me to take you right up to where your buddies were standing? Was there some special reason?"

David looked a bit embarrassed and finally said, "Well, Mom, I just didn't like that hat you were wearing the first day. It just didn't look like you. But yesterday you looked OK."

How we look really **does** make a difference!

IT'S A FAMILY SECRET! Loyalty is sort of an old-fashioned word that we don't hear very often anymore. And yet, how important it is in the lives of our children. As they learn loyalty within the family, they are training for future loyalty to their friends, their country, in their careers, and, far more important, loyalty to Jesus Christ.

The Living Bible paraphrases I Corinthians, chapter 13, verse 7 as: *"If you love someone you will be loyal to him no matter what the cost. You will always believe in him, always expect the best of him, and always stand your ground in defending him."*

Of course you know the faults of your husband and children (and they know yours!). But do you keep that knowledge within the family circle? Do you train your children to stand with their brothers and sisters in a crisis? Do they learn, because of your example, that family finances, family problems are **never** discussed with outsiders?

Remember, the Bible says **love covers.** [31]

TOGETHERNESS. Although we see this word often, we find there are many, many families that know little or nothing about being together as a family.

Through the years it has been an American tradition for the family to eat their meals together around a nicely-laid table. Children received their training in how to lay the table by doing it each day. Training in table manners was an important part of each meal.

TV FARE. Today, in many families, meals are planned around the TV set. So they have no table conversation because they have no dinner table! A TV tray and a TV dinner seem to have replaced the dinner table while a TV program takes the place of family conversation. "All rooms lead to TV" seems to be the slogan. Think of how many TV programs run counter to your Christian standards.

Have you realized what you, as a family, are missing by doing this? Those family conversations where you learned what happened during the day; what your children are thinking; with whom they are associating; what they are doing at school, are non-existent. No opportunity to train them in manners, conversation, etc. What a tragic loss.

FAMILY FUN. Wise parents will plan "fun times" for the whole family. These can be anything from toasting marshmallows around the fireplace to taking a trip to some interesting spot. These are the things of which memories are made and the experiences to which your children will look back as highlights of their youth.

A family I know made every holiday a "special" day. Everyone worked real hard the previous day to have the house "polished and shining" and no one worked on the holiday except, of course, to prepare meals! Sometimes it was a picnic in the back yard. Or a visit to points of interest in their own city which they had never seen. These occasions still supply happy memories for that family.

Our Marine Lieutenant told of the happy memories he has of Christmas at home.

On Christmas Eve, as various members of the family helped to trim the Christmas tree, Mother would read aloud from one of their favorite Christmas story books.

Early Christmas morning, the pajama-clad children trooped into their parents' bedroom for a time of singing Christmas carols and reciting the Christmas story from the Bible. Then came the opening of the gifts.

Later in the day, the family would visit some less-fortunate family in their area to take them food and gifts and to share the Bible Christmas story with them.

IMPROMPTU FUN TIMES can be great, too. Suddenly it's spring and you recall those springs when you went violet-picking. You share this excitement with the children and all start off to see if there is any place left where you could pick violets!

Or maybe you decide just to walk through the woods or park and see who can discover the most animals (squirrels, rabbits) or find the most unusual plant (watch out for that beautiful poison ivy!) or see the greatest variety of birds.

Ever try a hike through the snow? Or maybe it's just taking time to play a quiet game with the children.

Establishing those family traditions can create a wonderful family spirit. "How well I remember Easter mornings," a friend once remarked. "When we returned home from the Easter Sunrise Service in the park we always had a very special kind of coffee cake for breakfast and all the colored hard-boiled eggs we could eat!" The passing of time only makes such occasions more "special."

Whatever you do, build into the lives and characters of your children qualities of love and togetherness, of self-reliance, confidence, an awareness of the beautiful world around them and a consciousness of God in everything they see.

RECIPE FOR A HAPPY HOME

Perhaps you have seen the motto I have seen in many homes where I visit:

> CHRIST is the Head of this house,
> The unseen Guest at every meal,
> The Silent Listener to every conversation.

In the light of such a statement, are there any changes you would want to make in your home and family life?

The Bible says:

> *"WIVES, adapt yourselves to your husbands, that your marriage may be a Christian unity.*
>
> *HUSBANDS, be sure to give your wives much love and sympathy; don't let bitterness or resentment spoil your marriage.*
>
> *As for you*
>
> *CHILDREN, your duty is to obey your parents, for at your age this is one of the best things you can do to show your love for the Lord."* [32]

Because we care, we share the suggestions in this book in the hope that your family will be one of

GOD'S MASTERPIECES!

How
to Become
a Member of

God's
Forever Family

HERE'S HOW

Just as we are born into the human family, so we can be born into God's Family.

The Bible says: *"That which is born of the flesh is flesh; and that which is born of the Spirit is spirit."*

John 3:6

To be born into God's Forever Family,

1. you admit that you have sinned,

The Bible says: *". . .all have sinned and come short of the glory of God."*

Romans 3:23

2. you accept God's forgiveness,

The Bible says: *"If we confess our sins, He is faithful and just to forgive us our sins, and to cleanse us from all unrighteousness."*

I John 1:9

3. you invite Jesus Christ to come into your life.

The Bible says: *". . .as many as received Him, to them gave He power to become the sons of God, even to them that believe on His name. . ."*

John 1:12

You will become a member of God's Forever Family if you will pray sincerely as you invite Jesus Christ to come into your life.

MY PRAYER

Dear Lord Jesus,

I do believe that You are the Son of God and I want to be a member of God's Family.

Thank You for paying the penalty of sin for me. I willingly turn from my own way and accept Your forgiveness for all my past.

I invite You to come into my life right now and make me a child of God. From now on I want to know Your will for my life. Help me to follow You and to live to please You.

Thank You for giving me this new Life-that-shall-never-end.

In Jesus' name I pray. Amen.

Signed: _____

Date:_____

If you have prayed this prayer sincerely, on the authority of God's Word, you are now a Christian, a member of God's Family. We suggest that you sign your name and the date as a reminder of this moment when you prayed this prayer and received Jesus Christ as your Saviour and Lord. You should begin to read your Bible regularly (you will understand it better now) and communicate with God in prayer.

In the marriage ceremony, the bridegroom "takes" the bride and the bride "takes" the bridegroom and they become one. Each one commits himself/herself to the other for life.

So it is in God's realm. The Lord Jesus "takes" us to be His very own and we "take" Him to be our very own. We commit our lives to Him and He commits Himself to care for us. [33] Now we are rightly related to God.

Now we are Christians.

The Bible says: *"And this is the record, that God hath given to us eternal life, and this life is in His Son. He that hath the Son hath life; and he that hath not the Son of God hath not life."* [34]

Twenty centuries ago God stepped out of Eternity into Time in the person of His Son, Jesus Christ. He came to earth for a specific purpose:

...to pay the penalty for sin and
...to make it possible for us to be rightly related to God.

Jesus Christ lived a perfect life on earth for 33 years. Then He voluntarily gave His life and died on the cross for our sins.

To verify that He was the Son of God, three days after His death Jesus Christ came alive again!

Forty days later, He stepped back out of Time into Eternity where He lives today.

His mission was accomplished!

YOUR MARRIAGE A DISAPPOINTMENT?

Remember - God cares.

God will meet you right where you are.

Give Him all the tangled strands of your mixed-up life:

>your mistakes and frustrations. . .

>your longings and hopes. . .

>your heartaches and cares. . .

And let God smooth them out for you.

>Out of chaos, God will bring order.

>Out of ugliness, beauty.

>Out of turmoil, tranquility.

As you give God His rightful place, as Saviour and Lord of your life,

He will bring meaning and fulfillment to you.

>God will give you His peace.

Jesus said: *"...My own peace I give you. I do not give it to you as the world does. Do not be worried and upset; do not be afraid."*

John 14:27

WHERE TO FIND IT IN THE BIBLE

1. Genesis 2:18, 21, 22
2. Genesis 1:27,28
3. Genesis 2:24
4. John 2:1-11
5. Amos 3:3
6. II Corinthians 6:14a
7. I Corinthians 11:3
   and Ephesians 5:23
8. Ephesians 5:25
9. Proverbs 3:12 (Amplified)
10. Ephesians 6:4 (Phillips)
11. Deuteronomy 6:5-7 (Amplified)
12. Galatians 3:26-28 (Phillips)
13. Colossians 1:18b
14. I Peter 3:1,2 (Phillips)
15. Ephesians 4:15
16. Proverbs 31:12 (Amplified)
17. Ephesians 4:26
18. Hebrews 12:15 (Phillips)
19. Ephesians 4:32 (Phillips)
20. Hebrews 10:17
21. Matthew 6:14 (Phillips)
22. John 3:16

23. James 3:5,6 (Phillips)
24. I Corinthians 13:7, 8a (Phillips)
25. Proverbs 1:8
26. II Timothy 1:5 (Phillips)
27. Proverbs 22:6
28. Hebrews 12:6-9 (Phillips)
29. Proverbs 13:24 (NASB)
30. Psalm 18:35
31. Proverbs 10:12
32. Colossians 3:18-20 (Phillips)
33. Matthew 11:28
34. I John 5:11,12
